20TH CENTURY MEDIA

MEDIA

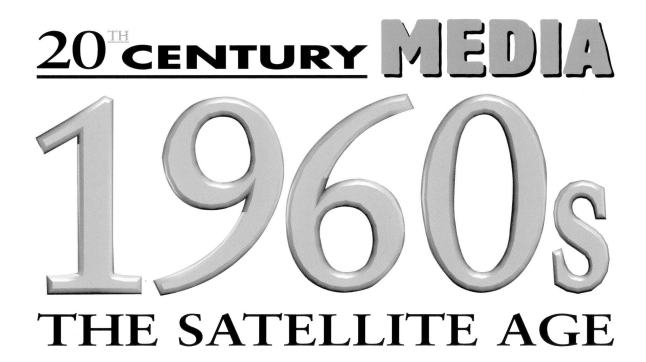

1960s

THE SATELLITE AGE

Please visit our web site at: www.garethstevens.com
For a free color catalog describing Gareth Stevens Publishing's
list of high-quality books and multimedia programs, call
1-800-542-2595 (USA) or 1-800-387-3178 (Canada).
Gareth Stevens Publishing's fax: (414) 332-3567.

Library of Congress Cataloging-in-Publication Data

Parker, Steve.
    20th century media / by Steve Parker.
        v. cm.
    Includes bibliographical references and index.
    Contents: [1] 1900–20: print to pictures. [2] 20s & 30s: entertainment for all.
 [3] 40s & 50s: power and persuasion. [4] 1960s: the Satellite Age. [5] 70s & 80s:
 global technology. [6] 1990s: electronic media.
    ISBN 0-8368-3182-9 (v. 1: lib. bdg.) — ISBN 0-8368-3183-7 (v. 2: lib. bdg.) —
 ISBN 0-8368-3184-5 (v. 3: lib. bdg.) — ISBN 0-8368-3185-3 (v. 4: lib. bdg.) —
 ISBN 0-8368-3186-1 (v. 5: lib. bdg.) — ISBN 0-8368-3187-X (v. 6: lib. bdg.)
    1. Mass media—History—20th century—Juvenile literature. [1. Mass
 media—History—20th century.] I. Title: Twentieth century media. II. Title.
 P91.2.P37   2002
 302.23'09'04—dc21   2002022556

This North American edition first published in 2002 by
Gareth Stevens Publishing
A World Almanac Education Group Company
330 West Olive Street, Suite 100
Milwaukee, Wisconsin 53212 USA

Designer: Rob Shone
Editor: James Pickering
Picture Research: Carrie Haines

Gareth Stevens Editor: Dorothy L. Gibbs

Photo Credits:
Abbreviations: (t) top, (m) middle, (b) bottom, (l) left, (r) right

The Advertising Archive Ltd.: page 17(b).
Corbis Stock Market: cover (bl), pages 6-7, 7(br, bl), 8(mr), 10(b), 19(tr), 20(b).
Hulton Archive: pages 4(t), 13(t), 14(l), 29(b).
Jasper Johns Collection © 2002 and the Estate and Foundation of Andy Warhol: page 20(t).
The Kobal Collection: pages 3, 24(both), 25(t, b).
Mirror Syndication International: pages 12(tr), 28(l).
NASA: cover (m), pages 6(bl), 8-9.
National Museum of Photography, Film, and Television/SSPL: page 22(tr).
Popperfoto: pages 4-5, 5(tr), 8(l), 9(bl, m), 12(b), 13(mr), 15(all), 16(tl), 19(b), 22(l, b), 23(tr), 26(bl), 28(br), 29(m).
Redferns: pages 11(br), 21(tr).
Rex Features/Alfred Eisenstaedt/Time Pix: page 28(tr).
Topham Picturepoint: page 11(t).
Vin Mag Archive Ltd.: pages 5(bm, br), 10(tr), 11(m), 17(t), 18(b), 25(m), 26(tr), 27(m); © Robert Crumb: page 27(r).

Printed in the United States of America

1 2 3 4 5 6 7 8 9 06 05 04 03 02

20TH CENTURY MEDIA

MEDIA

1960s

THE SATELLITE AGE

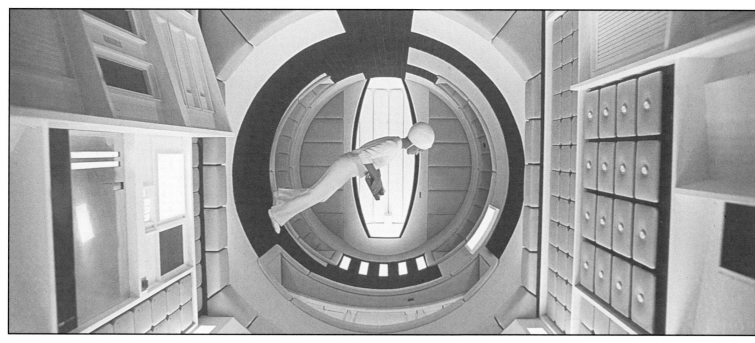

Steve Parker

Gareth Stevens Publishing
A WORLD ALMANAC EDUCATION GROUP COMPANY

CONTENTS

Some media experts predicted that television would mean the end of printed media, especially magazines.

The world was amazed at the news that the USSR had launched a man into space. Most people expected the USA to achieve this feat first.

NEW AND DIFFERENT

Mass media provide the entire world with news, views, information, and entertainment. By the 1950s, mass media included printed newspapers, magazines, books, and photographs, as well as the rapidly expanding broadcast media, radio and television. Movies, music, and art were important forms of mass media, too.

In the 1960s, television was the most exciting medium. It carried information in several forms, including both still and moving images, speech, music, and animation, and broadcasts could be updated in seconds. TV's impact was huge, especially on young people, who were always keen for things new and different. TV helped make the 1960s a decade of fast-changing styles in music, movies, theater, art, clothing — and even haircuts!

In 1964, the Beatles appeared in America on Ed Sullivan's top-rated variety show. Through the medium of television, this young British rock group reached millions and changed popular music in the United States overnight.

The first James Bond film came out in 1962. Yet in 2000, moviegoers and filmmakers voted "My name is Bond ... James Bond" the best-known line in movies.

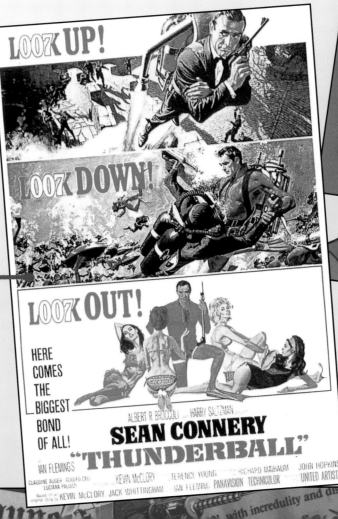

Artists, writers, and performers of the 1960s tested the boundaries of good taste, challenging censorship and the public's standards of decency.

ANOTHER WORLD

AEarly in 2000, people voted in a huge survey for the media moment of the 20th century. The result was the Apollo Moon landing on July 20, 1969. It was the first time anyone from Earth had walked on another world, and television broadcasted it — live!

Many newspapers delayed printing or produced special editions to publish reports and pictures of this epic event.

"THE *EAGLE* HAS LANDED"

The U.S. *Apollo 11* mission had blasted off on July 16. Upon reaching the Moon, crew members Neil Armstrong and "Buzz" Aldrin piloted the landing craft *Eagle* to the dusty Sea of Tranquillity. Touchdown was at 4:47 p.m., U.S. Eastern Daylight Time. Billions of people around the world sat glued to their television sets.

6

Apollo 11 crew members, (left to right) commander Neil Armstrong, Michael Collins, and Edwin "Buzz" Aldrin, all became instant celebrities when they returned to Earth on July 24.

Crew member Collins did not walk on the Moon. He stayed in orbit, in the command module Columbia, while Armstrong and Aldrin descended in the Eagle landing craft.

THE GREAT MOMENT

Reports that the Apollo astronauts radioed to Earth were accompanied by fuzzy television pictures of the Moon's surface. About six hours after Armstrong confirmed "The *Eagle* has landed," he climbed down the ladder of the landing craft to stand on the Moon's surface. The world watched, via a television camera attached to the *Eagle*. Armstrong's remark "That's one small step for man, one giant leap for mankind" has become one of the most famous quotes in history.

A TECHNICAL TRIUMPH

Landing on the Moon was an incredible technical achievement. So was showing it on live television. Using cables, radio links, and relatively new satellite technology to relay electronic signals back to Earth, and around the globe, had taken years of planning. Clearer, more detailed, still photographs, that had been taken by the astronauts, were also shared with the media.

In May 1961, U.S. president John F. Kennedy declared a goal to land a man on the Moon by the end of the decade and bring him safely back to Earth. Apollo's success gave the United States a huge boost in its space race with the USSR.

MOON-AD MADNESS

The Moon landing was the ultimate success of its time, and advertising immediately took up the theme. Images of rockets, astronauts, and spacecraft portrayed products, even everyday items such as coffee and laundry detergent, as the latest high-tech achievements. The aim of pictures and slogans used in the ads was to form a link in the minds of consumers between the product and the amazing Moon landing.

ood strong coffee s out of this world

There's nothing like a good strong coffee when you're feeling earthbound – ask the man on the moon. Pick up a coffee and it does the same for you.

Drink this coffee, and you, too, can go to the Moon!

SPACE TV

Live TV reports from around the world are nothing new today, but in 1960, beaming live television pictures across the globe was just a dream. Only two years later, however, a revolution in media technology made that dream come true. It began with the launch of *Telstar*, one of the world's first communication satellites.

LIMITED LINK

Telstar was the first satellite link between North America and Europe. It received TV signals from one side of the Atlantic; strengthened, or boosted, them; and sent them to the other side. Because of the way *Telstar* orbited Earth, it was in the correct position to function for only a limited time in each orbit. This period of time was called the transmission "window."

Telstar 1 *(above) was launched on July 10, 1962. The live television pictures it relayed from North America were received by the huge satellite dish* Arthur *(left) at Goonhilly in Cornwall, England.* Arthur *still receives TV signals today.*

A U.S. Delta rocket blasted off from Cape Canaveral, in July 1963, with the second of three experimental Syncom satellites, which were developed to test the idea of geosynchronous, or geostationary, orbits. Syncom 2 *was put in orbit high above the Equator over the eastern coast of Brazil.*

8

During space missions, ground stations around the world use large receivers to stay in touch with spacecraft, enabling Mission Control (above) to monitor the progress of the crafts at all times.

THE COMSAT CORPS

The aim of U.S.-based Communications Satellite Corporation, or Comsat, was to provide satellites for relaying radio and television signals and telephone calls. Formed in 1962, this new branch of the media business grew quickly. By 1965, Comsat had been renamed Intelsat, had fifteen member nations, and had sent more satellites into space.

NO MORE WINDOWS

Launched in April 1965, the *Early Bird* satellite, later renamed *Intelsat I*, solved *Telstar*'s problem of limited "windows." *Early Bird* was sent into a special type of orbit called geosynchronous, or geostationary, orbit (GO). When viewed from Earth, a satellite in GO seems to be standing still in space. Satellites in GO did not need tracking across the sky, and they were available every hour of every day. Two similar satellites, *Intelsat II* and *Intelsat III*, were launched in 1967 and 1969, completing a ring around Earth for instant, 24-hour, worldwide media links.

FIRST PICTURES FROM TELSTAR

Telstar 1 sent its live pictures, including this test image of the U.S. flag, only in black and white. Telstar 2 could relay color pictures.

9

A GOOD IDEA

The idea of satellites relaying signals for radio, TV, and telephone was first suggested in 1945. In a technical paper published by *Wireless World*, science-fiction writer Arthur C. Clarke explained that a satellite would be like a radio relay station on a very, very, very tall tower.

Arthur C. Clarke (b. 1917)

GO SATELLITES

The *Intelsat*s were put into geosynchronous, or geostationary, orbits called GOs, about 22,305 miles (35,890 kilometers) above the Equator. Each orbit takes exactly 24 hours. The Earth below spins at the same rate, so these satellites seem to hover, stationary, above Earth.

A transmitting dish sends signals to the satellite (uplink).

The satellite relays the signals to a receiving dish (downlink).

LIVE BY SATELLITE

The first generation of communication satellites could send live radio and television programs around the world in seconds, but the broadcast time on these new media links was limited and expensive. Which programs should be shown?

GLOBAL INTEREST

A satellite network needed programs of world-wide importance, so news was a major element. News programs concentrated on reports from North America, Europe, Japan, and Australia, all of which were regions that could receive the broadcasts and where many people had television sets. Another major programming element was sports. Fortunate timing enabled millions of TV viewers to watch the 1964 Olympic Games in Tokyo — live!

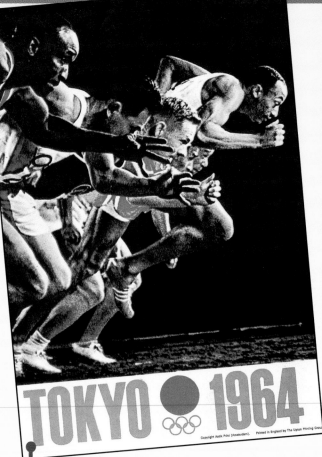

The Tokyo Olympics was relayed to North America by Syncom 3, *in orbit over the Pacific Ocean.* Relay 2 *sent them across the Atlantic to Europe.*

The lights, cameras, and microphones seen in this view of the CBS TV News studio during the U.S. presidential election in 1968 are vital pieces of equipment in the production of a television news broadcast.

10

Long before pay-per-view cable TV or Direct Broadcast Satellite TV brought international sports events to home viewers, the British Broadcasting Corporation (BBC) made a World Cup soccer championship available to all.

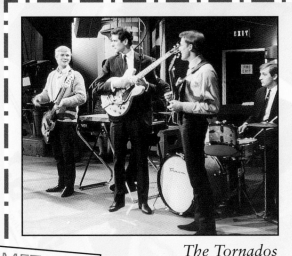

The Tornados

TELSTAR BECOMES A STAR

Global TV links amazed people, and "satellite fever" spread like wildfire. The satellites themselves became celebrities, with stories and songs written about them. In October 1962, the song "Telstar," by the Tornados, a British band, was No. 1 on the British charts. The song's eerie, echoing, organ sound captured the endless flight of a satellite in space. "Telstar" went to No. 1 in the United States, too, making the Tornados the first British group to top American charts.

JULES RIMET CUP
WORLD CHAMPIONSHIP
ENGLAND 1966 JULY 11-30
WEMBLEY · EVERTON · SHEFFIELD · SUNDERLAND · ASTON VILLA · MANCHESTER · MIDDLESBROUGH · WHITE CITY

FIFA

OFFICIAL SOUVENIR PROGRAMME
PRICE 2/6

COLORFUL MEXICO

In 1966, the world's second biggest sports event, the soccer World Cup, was televised live from England to more than fifty countries. The 1968 Olympics, televised from Mexico City, went a step further — the pictures were in color. During the 1960s, many people, especially in the United States, switched from black-and-white to color TV sets.

A live TV show that featured contributions from many different countries was televised to celebrate the second Intelsat "hook-up" in 1967. In London, the Beatles performed their latest hit single, "All You Need Is Love," to more than 300 million viewers.

11

MOLNIYA

Although the satellite revolution began in the West, the East was not idle. The USSR launched its first *Molniya*, which means "lightning," satellite in 1965. Because satellites in GO are always over the Equator, places to the far north and south of the planet have trouble receiving their signals. With much of the USSR so far north, *Molniya*s were designed to stay suspended over Russia through most of their 12-hour orbits. *Molniya*s worked in groups of three so that a satellite was always within range of the ground station.

PROGRAM WARS

Entertainment media, especially television, have responsibilities. Television captures large audiences with game shows, talk shows, "sitcoms" (situation comedies), and other light entertainment, but it also plays an important role in presenting more informative programming on history, world events, culture, and the arts.

THE FIGHT FOR VIEWERS

In the United States during the 1960s, some people felt that rivalry between the big networks was lowering program quality. While trivial variety shows, talk shows, comedy series, violence, and horror were increasing the number of viewers, were they also "dumbing down" the nation's education and intelligence?

The Ed Sullivan Show *was known for booking performers just as they were gaining great fame. In 1964, Sullivan presented the Beatles to 73 million U.S. TV viewers.*

The Beverly Hillbillies *comedy series topped TV ratings in the United States for two years of its 1961 to 1972 run.*

12

Johnny Carson took over as the host of NBC's Tonight Show in 1962. This late-night talk show, with its sly humor and celebrity guests, made Carson TV's highest-paid performer.

Before computer animation, TV shows with string puppets, such as Thunderbirds and Stingray, were hits.

ANOTHER NETWORK

In 1967, a Carnegie Commission report addressed TV broadcasting needs in the United States. It advised setting up a fourth national network, in addition to commercial-driven ABC, CBS, and NBC. The new network, the Public Broadcasting System (PBS), was formed from the many nonprofit cultural and educational TV stations already in existence across the nation. It was to be noncommercial, like Britain's BBC. Funding came from the government, private sources, and viewer donations.

MORE COMMERCIALS

In Britain, the opposite was happening. The state-funded BBC was being challenged by the commercial network, Independent Television (ITV). As the BBC began showing more programs with mass appeal, a second channel, BBC2, was added. Like PBS, BBC2 showed fewer mainstream programs and more on science, history, classical music, art, and literature.

EDUCATIONAL — BUT FUN!

Sesame Street, one of PBS's early hits, started in 1969. Produced by the Children's Television Workshop, it was aimed at the 3- to 5-year-old age group and focused on basic skills, such as learning to count. Cartoons, costumes, humor, puppets, and real children combined to make the program's educational content amusing.

Big Bird is one of Sesame Street's most popular and enduring characters.

WORLD NEWS

Every decade has momentous events that the media communicate around the world, but the 1960s seemed to have more than its fair share of dramatic news.

THE COLD WAR

In the 1960s, the Cold War was at its height. The capitalist United States and most Western European nations cherished democracy and freedom. The communist USSR and its Eastern allies preferred high levels of state control. Although the two superpowers never directly battled each other, they supported opposing sides in many regional conflicts, and they waged media campaigns against each other.

When U.S. president John F. Kennedy was shot and killed, on November 22, 1963, TV and radio news broadcasted reports within minutes.

THE POWER OF THE PRESS

One of the many differences between East and West was in their print media, known as "the press" from their production on printing presses. The West had many press agencies, and, as long as the facts were fairly accurate, each produced its own version of the news in its own style. The USSR's *Pravda*, which means "truth," was the only official Eastern news agency and newspaper, and its reports were under strict government control.

Communist governments, such as in Poland, tightly controlled articles in newspapers and magazines.

In capitalist nations, newspapers and other print media were subject to little state control.

THE BRINK OF NUCLEAR WAR

One of the most frightening events of the decade came in October 1962. The USSR had installed nuclear missiles on Cuba, a Caribbean island with a communist government. From Cuba, Soviet missiles could easily reach the United States. President John F. Kennedy sent U.S. warships to surround Cuba, and for the first time in the Cold War, the superpowers faced each other. For two weeks, the news media were full of terrible predictions of nuclear war. Then, Soviet premier Nikita Khrushchev agreed to withdraw the missiles. In return, the United States agreed to stop trying to weaken Cuba's communist government.

FUNNY — BUT SERIOUS

Unnerving events in the 1960s led to a revival in satire that ridiculed follies and pointless causes. Global nuclear war was one of the targets. What was the point of winning it when nuclear fallout would make most of the world uninhabitable?

British satirists (clockwise from top left) Peter Cook, Jonathan Miller, Alan Bennett, and Dudley Moore formed a group called Beyond the Fringe.

In August 1968, the USSR invaded Czechoslovakia. The Czech government had allowed reforms that loosened the grip of communism, and the Soviet Union was worried that other Eastern European nations might do the same.

Unarmed Czech citizens faced Soviet tanks on the streets. The communists quickly removed the Czech leader, Alexander Dubcek, from power and took back control of the country.

The Evening News

Red army machine-guns open up on Czechs

SOVIET INVADE THEN FIRING IN PRA

Wilson back in London calls up Johnson

S WINGING SIXTIES

Away from the wars and strife of global politics, the 1960s saw a huge change in popular culture. In the West, the social revolution of the 1950s continued. Young people were gaining even more time and money, but U.S.-inspired rock 'n' roll, black leather jackets, and blue jeans were already old-fashioned. The next generation wanted something new.

Disk jockeys had a strong influence on radio listeners. Here, British DJ Simon Dee (right) interviews pop singer Cliff Richard.

ENGLAND SWINGS

With fresh ideas on music, fashion, poetry, and art, London soon established itself as the new world capital of popular, or "pop," culture. Bands such as the Beatles and the Rolling Stones and fashion designers such as Mary Quant, who introduced the miniskirt, led a "British invasion." A new language developed with terms such as "groovy," "fab," and "swinging," which became the nickname for the whole decade — the Swinging Sixties.

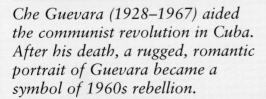

Che Guevara (1928–1967) aided the communist revolution in Cuba. After his death, a rugged, romantic portrait of Guevara became a symbol of 1960s rebellion.

CHE

THIRTY CENTS

JANUARY 3, 1964

TIME

MAN of the YEAR

THE WEEKLY NEWSMAGAZINE

MARTIN LUTHER KING JR.

VOL. 83 NO. 1

Martin Luther King, Jr.

A MATTER OF ATTITUDE

Through the media, especially music and television, ideas spread faster than ever before. With the new pop culture came different attitudes and morals that were significantly looser and more carefree than a decade earlier. Skirts were worn shorter, hair was worn longer, music was louder, and the use of nonmedical drugs became more open and widespread.

WHO'S THE MOST FAMOUS?

Stars of music, movies, and fashion became more famous than presidents, kings, and queens. In 1966, John Lennon, a member of the Beatles, was quoted as saying, "We're more popular than Jesus now." This casual remark, quoted out of context, was seized upon by some in the media as offensive. Especially in the southern United States, people protested by burning Beatles records.

MARTIN AND THE MEDIA

In spite of changing attitudes, the 1960s saw continuing struggles for civil rights, especially among racially oppressed people. Nowhere did the media report events in more detail than in the United States. Baptist minister Martin Luther King, Jr. (1929–1968) became a civil rights figurehead. His powerful and eloquent speeches against racial discrimination were covered by all forms of media, especially television. In 1964, King was awarded the Nobel Peace Prize and was *Time* magazine's Man of the Year. He was assassinated on April 4, 1968, in Memphis, Tennessee.

Daily Mirror

Drugs-trial quiz today, then final decision

4d.   Thursday, September 14, 1967   +   No. 19,820

U.S. BARS ROLLING STONE

TV team 'boards Caroline today'

By JAMES WILSON and KEVIN HUNT

A GRANADA television unit will board the pop pirate ship Radio Caroline today — despite all attempts to stop them.

A company spokesman said: "It is a secret plan and I cannot reveal how it will be done.

"But it will be done by a means which we believe to be legal."

It is thought that they may use a launch tug to put a team on board.

After filming material for "A World In Action" programme about Radio Caroline founder Ronan O'Rahilly, the team would be put ashore in Holland. Then they would be flown back to England.

Failed

The new plan was announced just after the trawler Ross Daleby berthed at Felixstowe, Suffolk, at 8.40 last night having failed to put a camera team on board the pirate ship.

Radio Caroline is one of two pirate ships still defying the government's anti-pirate radio law. The other is her sister ship, Radio Caroline North, off the Isle of Man.

The Ross Daleby's bid was called off — after a 36-hour wait at sea — when Granada bosses decided that the team might be committing a technical offence if they went aboard.

Granada television company were prepared to indicate on the interests of news gathering.

But the trawler's operators, J. Marr, Shipping Co. Limited, were . . .

THE HUNTERS

Five men of the TV film unit aboard the trawler Ross Daleby wave as a Daily Mirror chartered plane flies overhead.

Keith Richard in drama at airport

From BRIAN HITCHEN, New York, Wednesday

ROLLING STONE Keith Richard was refused entry to America when he arrived at Kennedy Airport here tonight.

Immigration officers took the pop guitarist to a private room and questioned him for more than half an hour before they announced their decision.

They agreed to allow him a "deferred entry" examination at the immigration offices on Broadway tomorrow morning.

The deferred entry examination means Richard must tomorrow answer questions about his drugs trial in Britain earlier this year.

Although he was denied official entry tonight, he was allowed to go to a New York hotel.

Expected

Richard arrived at Kennedy airport in a Trans-World jetliner with other Rolling Stones Bill Wyman, Brian Jones and Charlie Watts.

The group's lead singer Mick Jagger was expected to fly in later from Paris.

The Stones were due to see their New York-based manager Allen Klein.

An immigration spokesman said that a decision on Richard would be made tomorrow in the light of information requested from London.

Richard was sentenced to one year's imprisonment earlier this year for allowing his Sussex farmhouse home to be used for smoking Indian hemp.

Album

The conviction was later quashed and the sentence set aside by the High Court.

Jagger was sentenced to three months for possessing four drug tablets for an appeal he lost three months later.

Manager Klein said tonight: "The Rolling Stones aren't travelling in and out of America with a record album half-finished . . ."

Rolling Stone Keith Richard at London's . . . row Airport yesterday before flew to New . . .

POST
THE SATURDAY EVENING POST AUGUST 8–AUGUST 15 1964 25c

G.O.P. CAMPAIGN PREVIEW
NEW NOVEL ABOUT CHICAGO
BY SAUL BELLOW
SUMMER MADNESS:
THE BEATLES ARE BACK

Give drugs to addicts? / A $3 million mystery in the Bahamas / TV's comic cook

The British rock band Rolling Stones often had trouble with the authorities, including arrests for drug use, which put their U.S. tours in jeopardy. The Stones were defended, to a certain extent, by respected media figures such as William Rees-Mogg, editor of London's The Times.

The Beatles first visited the United States in February 1964. Their images appeared in every imaginable medium, whipping up the exciting chaos of "Beatlemania."

POP MUSIC

Popular music changed greatly during the 1960s — several times! At the beginning of the decade, the best-sellers were mainly rock 'n' roll, mushy ballads, and novelty songs. When the Beatles came along, in 1963, change gathered steam.

TRACKING TRENDS

Young people in the 1960s had more leisure time, more money, and more ways to learn about the latest trends. Television communicated both sounds and images of performers. New, specialized, pop music magazines delivered the latest information. Records, and the new cassette tapes introduced by Philips in 1963, were convenient and affordable music formats.

MUSIC STYLES

Among the many musical styles of the 1960s were the poetic folk and folk-rock songs of Bob Dylan, the California "surfin'" sound of the Beach Boys, and the soul harmony of Motown groups, such as the Temptations and the Supremes.

Transistor radios, conveniently powered by batteries, had shrunk to a size that could be carried almost anywhere. Many cars had radios, too. Some even had tape players.

18

CHANGING TIMES

British bands, including the Beatles, the Rolling Stones, and the Who, drew much early inspiration from musical styles in the United States, such as blues, soul, and rock 'n' roll. Later in the decade, more experimental musical styles evolved — the lilting peace anthems of the hippie movement, the wailing guitar sounds of Jimi Hendrix and Eric Clapton, and the heavy metal of Led Zeppelin and Deep Purple. Media journalists presented music and musicians in a serious, respectful way, as in the magazine *Rolling Stone*.

Rolling Stone devoted most of this 1969 issue to British musicians.

SONY
96
2×4 TRANSISTOR

ROLLING STONE
JUNE 14, 1969
No. 35
PETE TOWNSHEND
Jack Bruce   Roy Harper
Peter Green   Richie Havens
UK: 2/6
Chuck Berry
Jean-Luc Godard
The First British Issue!

GROUPS RULE

The Beatles, the Rolling Stones, and other bands of the mid-1960s changed not just musical styles but the whole music business. Previously, many top performers were solo singers with songs written and music played for them. The new bands wrote their own songs. They also played instruments and sang at the same time. They even produced their own recordings, sometimes, and their focus became albums rather than singles.

After the TV variety shows of the 1950s, pop music shows of the 1960s raced to the top of viewer ratings. One of the most popular music shows was Dick Clark's American Bandstand.

Pop music shows and other media products aimed at young people had been controlled by an older age group. The 1960s, however, brought younger hosts, producers, and performers, such as those on Jukebox Jury.

19

TV, radio, and publications for young people could encourage fan worship to an extreme degree. Crowds of teenagers followed their heroes, usually screaming and often weeping.

POP ART

Along with pop music came pop art. Artists of the 1960s offered more variety, and they experimented with many kinds of artistic media. Throwing off tradition, they produced art that was new, fresh, and different — although not necessarily serious or lasting.

CANS AND BOTTLES

Probably the best-known art celebrity of the time was Andy Warhol (1928–1987). After success as a New York commercial artist in the 1950s, Warhol developed a silk-screen process for printing large, bright photographic images on canvas. The images were repetitive, yet each one slightly different. His subjects ranged from movie stars and comic book heroes to soup cans and soft drink bottles.

Andy Warhol shunned traditional, "significant" art for pop culture, mass media images, such as his portraits of Marilyn Monroe. "In the future, everyone will be famous for fifteen minutes" was Warhol's memorable prediction.

Roy Lichtenstein's comic-like Whaam! *(1963) caused much controversy among art lovers who believed that works of art should be respectful, refined, serious, and unique. Pop artists wanted to avoid pretense and create closer links between art and everyday life.*

GIANT COMICS

Another influential U.S. artist was Roy Lichtenstein (1923–1997), who also based his bright, simplified art on mass-produced cartoons and comics. Unlike Warhol, however, Lichtenstein hand-painted his images, which were so enormous they looked almost abstract. Their lettering, speech balloons, and benday dots became Lichtenstein's most recognizable techniques.

SOFT SCULPTURES

Although pop art had actually started in the 1950s, the work of Warhol, Lichtenstein, Robert Indiana, James Rosenquist, George Segal, and others helped it spread around the world. Even sculptors played with the new methods and subjects of pop art. Using cloth and inflated plastic, Swedish-born Claes Oldenburg (*b.* 1929) produced giant "soft sculptures" of everyday hard objects, such as toilets and typewriters. Oldenburg also created huge hamburgers, slices of cake, and ice cream, works that raised smiles as well as questions among those who viewed them.

Photographer Michael Cooper and artist Peter Blake helped the Beatles create the cover of their album Sgt. Pepper's Lonely Hearts Club Band. *It reflected 1967's bright, brash, "Summer of Love."*

INFORMATION IMAGES

Because of TV, international publishing, and increasing long-distance air travel, people in the 1960s experienced more art and images from other cultures. Graphic designers used old styles and new techniques to produce clear, crisp, precise images that were easily understood around the world.

Crisp, clear, logo images for fashion (left), Olympic sports (below), wool garments (right), and petroleum products (above, right)

PHOTOJOURNALISM

Because pictures on a TV screen flash by so quickly, they are difficult to study in detail. Still photographs in newspapers, magazines, books, and other print media are not. Photography had other advantages over television, too.

Kodak's innovative Instamatic made photography simple.

In 1963, Buddhist monks, protesting against religious persecution, burned themselves alive in South Vietnam. Photographs like this one focused world attention on Southeast Asia.

SMALL AND FAST

TV cameras were huge and heavy and took a long time to set up. A stills camera, however, could capture images precisely in seconds. Some of the most powerful photos of the 1960s came from a devastating war in Southeast Asia — Vietnam. As photographers traveled with the troops in Vietnam, they took heart-stopping pictures of pain, death, and incredible destruction, including carpet bombings and napalm-fueled walls of fire.

Peace-lovers in the United States frequently faced the military in their endless protests against the Vietnam War.

22

Photojournalism exposed the reality of the dirty, deadly Vietnam War without glamour or romance.

PHOTOGRAPHS OF CONFLICT

The Vietnam War started with the Indochina War, when French troops fought communists under Ho Chi Minh. From about 1964, the United States supported South Vietnam against North Vietnamese communists, who used deadly guerrilla tactics in their jungle warfare. Photographs in newspapers and magazines brought the horrors of this conflict to the people of the United States and other Western nations, helping turn public opinion against the war.

IMAGES OF WAR

Photojournalists followed wars around the world, risking their lives to tell their stories in gripping images for magazines and newspapers. London-born Don McCullin (*b.* 1935), who photographed the suffering in Vietnam and many other hot spots, received the World Press Photographer award in 1964. Away from war, Diane Arbus, Lee Friedlander, and Gary Winogrand photographed details of daily routines, revealing poverty and aimless lives even in rich cities.

THE SLR CAMERA

Viewfinder — — Prism

Film — — Mirror

Focusing lens — — Light from image

On the move, most photographers used a small, light Single Lens Reflex (SLR) camera. Light from an image passes through the lens, reflects off of a mirror, and is twisted by a prism so the viewfinder shows exactly what the camera will record. When the picture is snapped, the mirror swings up for a split second, and light hits the film.

THE BIG SCREEN

Like other entertainment media, movies went through radical changes in the 1960s. Although great attention was paid to the costumes, scenery, and set designs, content could be confusing or trivial. Style was often more important than substance.

In 2001: A Space Odyssey *(1968), Arthur C. Clarke's science-fiction story of "ape to spaceman," U.S. director Stanley Kubrick used a rambling, confusing mass of hypnotic special effects that established a new film style.*

French director François Truffaut (1932–1984) explored film styles such as future fiction, in Fahrenheit 451 *(1966), and the dark suspense of film noir, in* The Bride Wore Black *(1968).*

NEW WAVE

During the 1950s, the big U.S. film studios in Hollywood had suffered from both the growth of television and the campaigns against the supposed communist takeover of the entertainment business. "New Wave" filled the gap with downbeat, personal stories filmed on location rather than in studios. New Wave films began in France and included works such as *Jules et Jim* (1962), directed by François Truffaut; *La Femme Infidèle*, or *The Unfaithful Wife*, (1968), directed by Claude Chabrol; and *La Chinoise*, or *Chinese Lady*, (1967), directed by Jean-Luc Godard.

THE FEEL-GOOD FACTOR

Depressing dramas, such as *Saturday Night and Sunday Morning* (1960), about working-class people trying to cope with day-to-day existence, yet rebel against authority, were a trend in British films. Offsetting this gritty realism and restoring some glamour, excitement, and feel-good escapism to movies, agent 007, aka James Bond, made his first appearance in *Doctor No* (1962).

HOLLYWOOD REVIVAL

As Hollywood was recovering, U.S. filmmakers turned to detailed studies of the traditions and conventions of society. Their movies reflected more liberal lifestyles, as in *The Graduate* (1967), *Midnight Cowboy* and *Easy Rider* (1969), and the profoundly anti-Vietnam War film *M*A*S*H* (1970). *Bonnie and Clyde* (1967) was a milestone in film, mixing graphic, yet casual, violence with acid humor.

Actor Dustin Hoffman shot to fame as an awkward, downtrodden, college graduate trapped in a middle-class world of shallow values and hypocrisy.

MOVIE RATINGS

As filmmakers of the 1960s experimented with greater levels of sex, violence, and horror, many countries set up rating systems to indicate the type of content in each movie. The United States established the Motion Picture Rating System in 1968.

The Production Code, which was written in 1930, was replaced by the rating system.

X — Adults only

Universal (suitable for all)

Suitable for older children

James Bond movies combined high adventure, exotic locations, clever gadgets, humor, and action.

LOOK UP! LOOK DOWN! LOOK OUT!

HERE COMES THE BIGGEST BOND OF ALL!

ALBERT R. BROCCOLI · HARRY SALTZMAN

SEAN CONNERY "THUNDERBALL"

IAN FLEMING'S

KEVIN McCLORY · JACK WHITTINGHAM · TERENCE YOUNG · RICHARD MAIBAUM · JOHN HOPKINS · PANAVISION TECHNICOLOR · UNITED ARTISTS

Easy Rider is a film about two freedom-loving motorcyclists with hippie values and shiny, chrome "choppers," crossing the USA to a rock music sound track.

IN PRINT

The media of printed words need no costly gadgets or electronic communication. They need only the writer, the printed piece, the reader's eyes — and imagination. Many of the most unusual and least traditional ideas of the 1960s were introduced in print.

COUNTERCULTURE

As in other decades, many writers wanted to make their marks by moving in new directions. In the mid-1960s, a counterculture developed, rejecting the traditions of settled family life, daily routines, hard work, and respect for authority. Nonviolent rebellion was in the air, and artists, musicians, and performers quickly joined in. The new catchwords were "peace" and "love."

The novel A Clockwork Orange *(1962), by British author Anthony Burgess (1917–1993), tells of a bleak future in which violent criminals are brainwashed by what seems to be an even more violent society.*

Editors of the British student magazine Oz, (left to right) James Anderson, Richard Neville, and Felix Dennis, challenged standards of decency and were convicted in an obscenity trial in 1971.

BREAKING OUT

Some writers felt restricted by literary conventions such as keeping fiction and nonfiction separate. U.S. authors Tom Wolfe, Hunter S. Thompson, Joan Didion, and Norman Mailer began to mix styles, describing real events using the flowery techniques of storytelling. This fresh approach was known as New Journalism. It had many spin-offs into other media, including music, poetry, films, painting, and sculpture. These art forms were often combined into multimedia events known as "happenings."

An artist's impression of Tom Wolfe

TOM WOLFE

U.S. author Tom Wolfe (b. 1931) was a leader of New Journalism. With a sharp, lively style, his journalistic works reported details of daily life but with the colorful descriptions and exaggerations used in novels. One of his best-known works, *The Electric Kool-Aid Acid Test* (1968), was about early hippie culture. Wolfe went on to write one of the best-selling books of the 1980s, *Bonfire of the Vanities*.

"Underground" cartoonists, such as Robert Crumb (b. 1943), lent humor to difficult, often taboo, or dangerous subjects. Crumb's *Zap Comix was first published in 1968.*

CATCH-22

Authors used satire to show that authority is often pointless, even stupid. In Joseph Heller's *Catch-22* (1961), the character Yossarian, who is in the U.S. Air Force during World War II, tries to avoid flying dangerous missions by saying he is insane. The fact, however, that Yossarian recognizes the missions are dangerous shows that he *is* sane. It is an argument that goes around and around — a Catch-22.

Mad *magazine began in 1952 and was especially popular with teenagers. In comic-book disguise, it poked serious fun at the rich and famous.*

PRINTING WITH LIGHT

Traditional printing, called letterpress, used pieces of metal with raised lines that formed the shapes of the letters. To make a printing plate, they were coated with ink and pressed onto paper. In phototypesetting, which is much faster, the letters are dark shapes on clear film. Light is shined through letter shapes on a disk, building the required words, a letter at a time, and forming a kind of photograph printing plate.

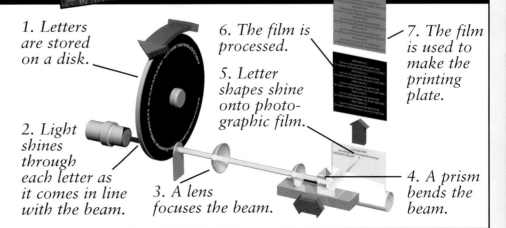

1. Letters are stored on a disk.

2. Light shines through each letter as it comes in line with the beam.

3. A lens focuses the beam.

4. A prism bends the beam.

5. Letter shapes shine onto photographic film.

6. The film is processed.

7. The film is used to make the printing plate.

TECH TROUBLES

The 1960s had been a decade of high-tech achievements, especially in space, from the first Russian astronaut, Yuri Gagarin, in 1961 to the Apollo Moon landing in 1969. The new jumbo jets also took their first flights in 1969. Back on Earth, however, problems were mounting.

In 1967, the supertanker Torrey Canyon *broke up in a storm, coating the coasts of southwestern England with thick, suffocating oil.*

Rachel Carson (1907–1964) was a marine biologist.

Daily Mirror

Wilson calls a 'beach battle' Cabinet

4d   Monday, March 27, 1967   No 19,673

The "beach battle" Cabinet from the left: Mr. Maurice Foley, Sir Elwyn Jones, Mr. Roy Jenkins, Mr. Harold Wilson, Mr. Anthony Greenwood and Mr. Gerry Reynolds.

SHATTERED TANKER BREAKS UP IN GALE

'Oil is spewing from her tanks'

THE grounded oil tanker Torrey Canyon began to break up last night. The ship's back split in two, and the bow and stern sank under water.

A Royal Navy helicopter pilot said: "My guess is that neither part will be there tomorrow morning. They will both have sunk."

The captain of the salvage tug Utrecht radioed that the Torrey Canyon must be considered lost.

Oil began gushing from the tanker faster than at any time since the wreck last Saturday, when the ship crashed on to the Seven Stones reef, twenty miles from Land's End.

This menace to Britain's South Coast seaside resorts is now greater than ever.

The new mass of oil may prove to be virtually indestructible.

OFF TO A RACING START

THE HORROR IN A QUIET HARBOUR

This is the harbour at the Cornish holiday town of Porthleven. Swirling up to the sea wall is ugly black muck of oil from the ill-fated tanker Torrey Canyon. Already at least sixty miles of beaches are hit just as badly. And now the worst-ever crisis to hit beaches of Britain grows each hour.

POLLUTION PROBLEMS

Although daily life was becoming easier and more convenient, people, especially in wealthy Western nations, were beginning to recognize several inter-related problems. The growing numbers of cars on the highways and factories churning out consumer products were creating polluting chemicals and piles of waste. With the use of nuclear power stations and the looming threat of nuclear war, radioactive pollution was also a fear.

Members of the Campaign for Nuclear Disarmament (CND) held "Ban the Bomb" protests in many cities on a regular basis. The goal of these protests was to rid the world of the nuclear weapons that could destroy it or make it impossible to inhabit.

28

FUTURE DISASTER?

In 1962, Rachel Carson portrayed a terrible vision in her book *Silent Spring*. It gathered evidence from many sources to predict a future where no birds hatched from eggs to sing in springtime, where fruit trees were bare in autumn, and where animals and people died from mysterious illnesses. Such events were caused by the growing use of chemicals, especially DDT and other pesticides, that accumulated in the environment and harmed living things.

ACCIDENTAL AND DELIBERATE

In a series of famines, plagues, and ecological disasters, supertankers spilled giant oil slicks into the sea, devastating marine life. Behind the Aswan High Dam, built on Egypt's Nile River for hydroelectricity and irrigation, a huge lake submerged vast areas of wildlife. In medicine, germs were developing resistance to the antibiotic "wonder drugs." The media helped identify these problems and bring them to the attention of a wider public, leading to protests and events such as the first Earth Day on April 22, 1970.

THE GREEN REVOLUTION

The late 1960s saw the growth of the "Green Movement," activists concerned about protecting nature, reducing pollution, and cutting the sky-rocketing rate of using resources such as coal, oil, metals, and wood. In the 1970s, the Green Revolution would very rapidly gain momentum.

Besides drowning wildlife, the lake behind the Aswan High Dam flooded sites of historical interest, such as the ancient temples at Philae. International efforts helped move people and some treasures to safety.

In 1967, people in southeastern Nigeria claimed their land as the new country Biafra. Through the media, the world watched as famine and civil war killed a million people. By 1970, Nigeria had regained control.

TIME LINE

	WORLD EVENTS	HEADLINES	MEDIA EVENTS	TECHNOLOGY	THE ARTS
1960	•U.S.: Kennedy elected president •USSR: Brezhnev becomes president	•U.S. spy plane captured by USSR •"The Twist" dance craze goes global	•U.S.: Kennedy-Nixon debates on live TV	•U.S. launches first experimental communication satellite, Echo I	•Alfred Hitchcock: Psycho •Lerner & Lowe: Camelot
1961	•Bay of Pigs invasion of Cuba •OPEC formed	•Russian cosmonaut Yuri Gagarin is first person in space •Wall separates East and West Berlin	•Russian ballet dancer Rudolf Nureyev defects to West	•Bell Laboratories tests communication by light waves •IBM Selectric "golf ball" typewriter	•Joseph Heller: Catch-22 •Claes Oldenburg opens "The Store"
1962	•Cuban missile crisis •Algeria gains independence from France	•Marilyn Monroe dies •Georges Pompidou becomes prime minister of France	•Walter Cronkite starts as anchorman on CBS Evening News (to 1981)	•Telstar 1 communication satellite launched •Comsat Corporation formed	•Doctor No (agent 007's first movie) •François Truffaut: Jules et Jim
1963	•Nuclear Test Ban Treaty signed by USSR, UK, and USA	•President John F. Kennedy assassinated •Buddhist monks in Vietnam burn themselves alive	•Jack Ruby murders Lee Harvey Oswald on live TV	•Syncom 2 satellite launched into geo-stationary orbit •Audiocassette tapes first introduced	•Lichtenstein: Whaam! •Beach Boys "surfin'" sound hits pop music charts
1964	•UN sanctions against South Africa •Vietnam War begins •PLO formed	•Martin Luther King, Jr. wins Nobel Peace Prize •Britain's Beatles are a huge hit in U.S.	•Tokyo Olympics seen globally on TV, live, by satellite •Beatles appear on The Ed Sullivan Show	•U.S.: first prime-time TV broadcasts in color •BASIC programming introduced	•Walt Disney: Mary Poppins •Topol stars in Fiddler on the Roof
1965	•End of capital punishment in UK •India and Pakistan at war	•Black rights activist Malcolm X assassinated •Singapore gains independence from Malaysia	•UK: state funeral for wartime prime minister, Winston Churchill	•Early Bird (Intelsat I) communication satellite launched into geostationary orbit	•Sonny & Cher: I Got You Babe •Rolling Stones: I Can't Get No Satisfaction
1966	•Cultural Revolution in China	•USSR lands unmanned space probe on Moon •Indira Gandhi becomes India's first woman prime minister	•Beatle John Lennon's "We're more popular than Jesus" quote	•Fiber optic cable •Xerox markets Telecopier fax machine	•The Monkees TV series begins •Bob Dylan: Blonde on Blonde
1967	•Six-Day War between Arabs and Israelis •Biafra declares independence from Nigeria	•Our World live TV show links countries around the world	•"Summer of Love" peace demonstrations and "love-ins" •BBC starts Radio 1 for younger listeners	•IBM invents the floppy disk •Cordless telephones introduced	•Andy Warhol: Marilyn •McLuhan: The Medium Is the Message •Rolling Stone magazine founded
1968	•USSR invades Czechoslovakia •Student riots in Paris •Vietnam: Tet Offensive	•Martin Luther King, Jr. assassinated •Robert Kennedy assassinated	•U.S.: violent antiwar demonstrations at Chicago's Democratic National Convention	•Olympics in Mexico City televised live, in color, by satellite	•Stanley Kubrick: 2001: A Space Odyssey •Hair (hippie-style rock musical on Broadway)
1969	•British troops sent to Northern Ireland •Stonewall Uprising starts Gay Rights movement	•Apollo 11 astronauts land on Moon •Rock festival held in Woodstock, New York	•First words broadcasted from the Moon •France: first flight of Concorde supersonic jet	•UCLA and Stanford computers exchange data in early form of Internet communication	•X-rated Midnight Cowboy wins Best Picture Oscar

GLOSSARY

benday: a photoengraving technique using dots of color to create shading, texture, and tone.

Cold War: the rivalry between the democratic United States and the communist Soviet Union, from about 1950 to 1990, that involved no direct military action and did not sever diplomatic relations.

counterculture: a faction, or part of a society, upholding values and beliefs that strongly contrast with those of the established society.

geosynchronous (geostationary) orbit: the path of a satellite around Earth, high above the Equator, traveled in the same amount of time as Earth's daily rotation so that, from Earth, the satellite appears to be standing still, or stationary.

location: a place outside of a production studio that has the appropriate look and surroundings for filming scenes in a particular movie or TV program.

network: a large group of radio or TV stations that broadcast the same programs simultaneously over a wide area.

New Wave: a movement in the history of motion pictures that often used experimental photographic techniques to produce films that tended to be abstract or symbolic.

photojournalism: the technique of presenting news using mostly photographs with captions, rather than full text with only a few photographs.

satire: the use of biting wit or humor and ironic language to mock or ridicule the faults and failings of people, organizations, and institutions, especially those with great power and influence.

studio: a large room equipped for producing and broadcasting radio and television programs. Also, the general name for a large motion picture company.

MORE BOOKS TO READ

The 1960s: From the Vietnam War to Flower Power. Decades of the 20th Century (series). Stephen C. Feinstein (Enslow)

1960s: Space and Time. 20th Century Science and Technology (series). Steve Parker (Gareth Stevens)

Andy Warhol. Getting to Know the World's Greatest Artists (series). Mike Venezia (Children's Press)

The Beatles. Trailblazers of the Modern World (series). Michael Burgan (World Almanac® Library)

The Cold War. 20th-Century Perspectives (series). David Taylor (Heinemann)

First on the Moon. I Was There (series). Barbara Hehner (Hyperion Press)

The History of Motown. African American Achievers (series). Virginia Aronson (Chelsea House)

Kennedy Assassinated! The World Mourns: A Reporter's Story. Wilborn Hampton (Candlewick Press)

Martin Luther King, Jr. The Importance of (series). John F. Wukovits (Gale Group)

Satellites. Inventors & Inventions (series). Mary Virginia Fox (Marshall Cavendish)

WEB SITES

All About Earth Day.
 earthday.wilderness.org/history

Sixties British Pop Culture.
 www.sixtiespop.com

TV's All the Rage!
 4the60s.4anything.com/4/0,1001,6827,00.html

What Happened in the Sixties?
 www.bbhq.com/sixties.htm

Due to the dynamic nature of the Internet, some web sites stay current longer than others. To find additional web sites, use a reliable search engine with one or more of the following keywords: *Apollo 11, British invasion, Cold War, Earth Day, Martin Luther King, Jr.,* Molniya, *pop art, public television,* Telstar, *Vietnam War,* and *Andy Warhol.*

INDEX